Building Your Chambered Wood Surfboard

Second Edition

A complete guide to building a chambered wood surfboard using cedar two by fours or similar stock. This book includes layout, assembly, shaping, and chambering instructions to build your own 8' CedarGlide® Mini Longboard.

By Chad Stone

Copyright 2011 by Chad Stone/Timeless Surf Company.com
All rights reserved.
ISBN: 978-1-105-08784-4

!!DISCLAIMER!!

Working with wood is dangerous. Working with tools is even more dangerous. DO NOT do anything to hurt yourself or that will cause any kind of danger to you or anyone, or anything else. This guide is simply a compilation of ideas that I use to make a surfboard, and it should be used accordingly. It is not intended to be utilized by anyone or anything for any purpose other than reading amusement. By reading this compilation, you are taking full responsibility for your actions and hold me, my company, and everyone and everything in the world, NOT responsible for anything and everything that may or may not happen, to anyone or anything. Ever. It is a shame that I have to say this.

Introduction

Building a wooden surfboard is nothing new. The first known surfboards were carved from timber, as this was the preferred construction material for many years, and these days wooden surfboards are making a huge comeback due to their nostalgic look, classic glide, and "green" construction method. The extra weight makes these surfboards very smooth and graceful in the water, and produces abundant drive and speed. Oh, and they *look* great too!

I have built many boards using different materials and construction methods and have since been helping others build their own treasures by offering these books. This particular method describes a very classic way of building hand-tooled wooden surfboards with a few modern ideas and a slew of tips and tricks to make the process easy for the beginner using just a few tools, or the handyman who has everything. I highly recommend having your board glassed professionally and I will not provide much info on glassing in this book, as glassing is an art in itself! I tried to address all variations and ideas in this book so you can create a shapeable blank, whether you are using my plans or just winging it and creating your own model.

All of these techniques and ideas have been combined to produce a board that is as fun and rewarding to build as it is to ride. They are more rigid and durable than most modern surfboards and, with proper care they will be a truly **_Timeless_** design than can be cherished for many, many years.

Contents

Pg.	Topic
1	Material List
3	Selecting Lumber
5	Cutting the Rocker
6	Make a Plan - Chambering
7	Layout and Tacking
8	Cutting the Rocker (Diagram)
11-13	Truing Your Blank
13-14	Roughing the Rails
15	Break It Up
16-17	Chambering (Diagram)
19	Together Again
21	Leash Plug/Vent
22	A Word about Rails
23-24	A Word about Fins
25	Links
26	Closing

Materials & Equipment

Choosing the right wood:

Choosing wood is one on the most important and defining steps in building your wooden surfboard. Be sure to select boards that are nice and straight as you look down the wide side of the lumber. The boards can have a bend as rocker and can actually fit this project better, with less waste wood since the rocker needs to be cut in regardless. You will also find huge differences in the weight of similar boards depending on the density and moisture content. Try to find the lightest lumber if possible, a little bit of weight is ok, but these boards can get heavy real quick! Since you will be cutting the rocker in each board before you glue and shape them, there are certain areas of each piece that can have blemished or knots, these area will be cut off and won't affect the final outcome.

That said, when inspecting board stock, be sure that the areas that will be used are free of splits, knots, rot, bug holes, and other undesired blemishes. Some of these blemishes, when places properly in the layout, can create great effects, but they can also make shaping the board a nightmare. Loose knots can dislodge while planing and leave large gaping holes in your project. Bug or worm holes can make nice natural trenches that look super rustic when finished, but when you glass the board, these can leave air bubbles, drink lots of resin, or even leave valleys in the finish since the wood doesn't well the same as untainted wood. Take your time, sometimes it takes several visits to several stores for several months to find the right stock.

Don't be in a hurry to be a failure! Find the right pieces for your project. I have found that indoor lumberyards in my area have much nicer stock and the lumber is usually drier and straighter than those that sit out in the rain and humidity. I have not experimented with other woods for this construction method, though I am sure that redwood, paulownia, Balsa, Spruce, or Douglas Fir would work. Hardwoods such as Oak and Maple could be used, but it might turn out to be *VERY* heavy.

A word about glues:

There are millions of different types and brands of glue available and it can be hard to decide which one is best for this job. I highly recommend using Gorilla Glue since it is water-PROOF, expands to fill any gaps in construction, and cures very rigid. Standard wood glues can be used but they are only "water resistant", and they do not cure as strong as the Gorilla glue. I have heard of folks using Liquid Nails or PL construction glue with good results, but in my experience it was too "pliable" much like caulk and allowed some seams to creep a bit.

Epoxy glues would be the supreme adhesive, except that it can get pricey and the application is a little bit more of a chore. It must be mixed properly, spread efficiently, and secured quickly. Be sure to wear rubber gloves when using these more powerful glues!! It is very difficult to wash off and will leave black spots on your hands that won't peel off for a good 2 days!

Tools:

You are only as good as the tools you are working with. You can find out the hard way (like I did) or take my word for it. A cheap scroll saw will give you wiggly wobbly cuts, and dull blades will just make the work harder for you and more dangerous! I just upgraded to a nice solid DeWalt tool setup, and I cannot believe the difference in workability! Be sure to get a nice set-up and keep you tools clean and sharp. You'll be glad you did.

Notes

Lumber Needed

(15) Cedar 2x4s x Board length
 * or anything combination of thicknesses as long as they add up to 23" when they are all glued together.

Tools

(1) bottle of Elmers white glue or similar
(2) Large bottles of Gorilla Glue or similar.
Various hole saws, OR router bits, OR forstner bits for chambering (be careful!!!)
Jigsaw or large band saw
Electric Planer Or Belt Sander
Block plane/spoke shave
At least (4) 24' bar clamps (more is always better)
Various grit sandpaper
Tape measure or yardstick
Straightedge
Pencil
Spray bottle
Fin box (if you are not glassing your fin on)
Leash plug (if you are not making your own)
Patience!!

Get your Blueprints

Email me @ TimelessSurfCo@Gmail.com (Subject: Chambered Blueprints) to request your free set of downloadable blueprints for the 8' Cedar Glide Mini Longboard. You can take the file to your local print shop to get it printed out and then you will be ready to go.

Cutting the Rocker
(see illustration on pg 8)

Now that you have selected the PERFECT lumber for your surfboard, it's time to start cutting. If your stock is rough sawn or has small blemishes that need to be removed, now is a good time to run them through your planer. After the rocker is cut, the boards will have more of a tendency to "roll" when planing. I use a bench plane to get my stock finished to a smooth, uniform surface. Rough sawn lumber will leave small crevices in the seams, which can make the glue bonds weak.

After you have them finished to your liking, you can take the plans that you bought (or ones you made) and transfer them to a piece of stock. A piece of ½ " plywood or a 1x4 would work fine for a master template to keep for future projects, or just glue it to your first 2x4 and use that as a master. Just use white glue, paste, or spray adhesive to attach the blueprints right to the face of the board. Now take your time and use a good quality tool to cut the rocker each piece of wood. This is the monotonous part of the build, doing the same thing 15 times in a row isn't a whole lot of fun but it has to be done, so get going.

A large band saw would be optimal, but the pieces can also be cut out using a handheld jigsaw if you aren't blessed with abundant tooling. It is best to cut the pieces just a little large to give you more stock to square the blank up once it is glue together, unless you can cut a perfect, square line without wobbles or deviations. Be careful not to cut your rocker too thin though! Even a small dip in a board can be an eyesore in the finished product. Once you get all of the pieces cut to the rocker shape, take a break, go surf. You have to get all that sawdust off of you somehow!

Plan Ahead

When it comes down to building your new board, you now have a quite few options to choose from. Here are 3 different, equally viable ways to glue these boards together.

Tack and Chamber

The idea here is to tack the boards together with small glue dots to create a "blank", cut the outline, square up the blank and rough shape the board. Next we will break the boards apart, releasing the small glue tacks, so we can chamber each board individually to make them lighter, then glue them back together and finish the shape. Legend has it that this method was developed by non-other than Jim "The Genius" Phillips and is the best way to shed weight. Although it is time consuming, it is worth every second of labor. This method will be covered in detail in this book as the other methods or just stripped down versions of this.

Pre-Camber and Glue

Here, you would clamp your stock together and mark your outline. The boards can now be chambered, but you must leave lots of stock especially toward the edges and rails. This method has more of a tendency to fail since you never know how much stock is in each section, plus the finished product usually weighs more than the previous method. Or you might just take off too much stock, exposing a chamber so be careful!!

Just Glue-it

If you are using super light wood or if you don't care about weight, you can simply glue the pieces together and shape it. Easy enough right?!? Sure, but you might end up with an 80 pound surfboard!

Layout and tacking

Now that the rocker is cut in each board, you can start laying the boards out and tack them together to form your blank. Lumber with blemishes on the ends can be used toward the outside of the blank so that the blemishes will be removed when the outline is cut. Now let's mock the pieces together. This is where you can get creative, stacking the boards to create different grain patterns or effects. Once they are laid out to your preference, number or label each board so you can remember where they go. Be sure to mark them on a section that won't be cut or planed off and remember to re-mark them if they *do* get sanded off before the outline is cut. After that, only the middle pieces will be interchangeable.

Tack it up

Starting with the center boards, glue all the pieces together, two at a time. This gives you plenty of time to align each piece *just right* before the glue bonds. Be aware of any imperfections and their position in relation to the finished outline. Grab your bottle of white glue and place a small dab (about the size of a BB) every 2 feet or so down the length of one board and clamp it to its neighbor. Keep your glue in the center of the boards (mid rocker), where the chambers will be cut out and about 1" from the end of the board. If the glue is too close to the edges it will almost definitely split when you try to release the bond later to chamber the wood. Too much glue also makes it very difficult to pull apart later, causing splits and cracks, so remember, even that small drop you place on the board will spread into a large glob when you clamp it and you can always add a bit more glue later if your boards come apart too soon, so use the glue sparingly. Clamp the boards together with your bar clamps and allow the glue to dry for an hour or so before gluing the next pair. Take your time.

Cut your outline (see illustration on page 9 & step 1 on page 14)

Now you should have a big, heavy blank that you can barely manage! Let's start cutting some of the stock off so it's a bit easier to handle. First, find the center line of your board and mark a line down the length. Next, make a line on each side of the blank marking the final desired finished width (usually between 22-24"). See your plans for the suggested finished width. Your plans include a nose and tail template that now needs to be transferred to your blank. You will need to either transfer the shape to your blank directly or glue them to a piece of stock to be used as a master template for future projects. Set the nose template on the nose of the board so that the template corner line up with the center line that you marked, then pivot the template from this point until the aft side of the template meshed well with the OUTSIDE (width) mark that you measured earlier. Flip the template and mark the other side of the nose the exact same way. Not too shabby!

Next, do the same with the tail side of the template. Remember, you can always deviate from these plans or even wing it if you are so bold, just keep is symmetrical.

You can now rough in your outline with a jigsaw or whatever tool that you deem worthy, cutting just outside of your marks in order to keep some extra stock on the blank; you can trim and smooth it out later. Cut out one side and use the cut piece to double check your layout on the opposite side. Does it look ok? Well, cut it out then! If not, remark your lines and get going. The middle section of your board will then be feathered into the nose, flowing to your width marks, and finally feathered back into the tail outline. Cool, now you shed about 30% of the weight from this tank AND it is starting to resemble a surfboard. Well done.

Cutting the Rocker/ Assembly

Grab a board (or master template stock)

Transfer the blueprints

Cut it out (leave extra stock)

* Use this peice to transfer the rocker to the next piece of stock, repeat 15+ times!

Glue it (small drops!!)

Clamp it

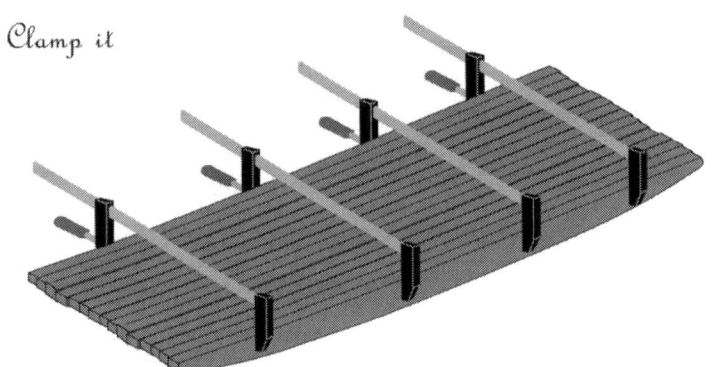

Marking the Outline

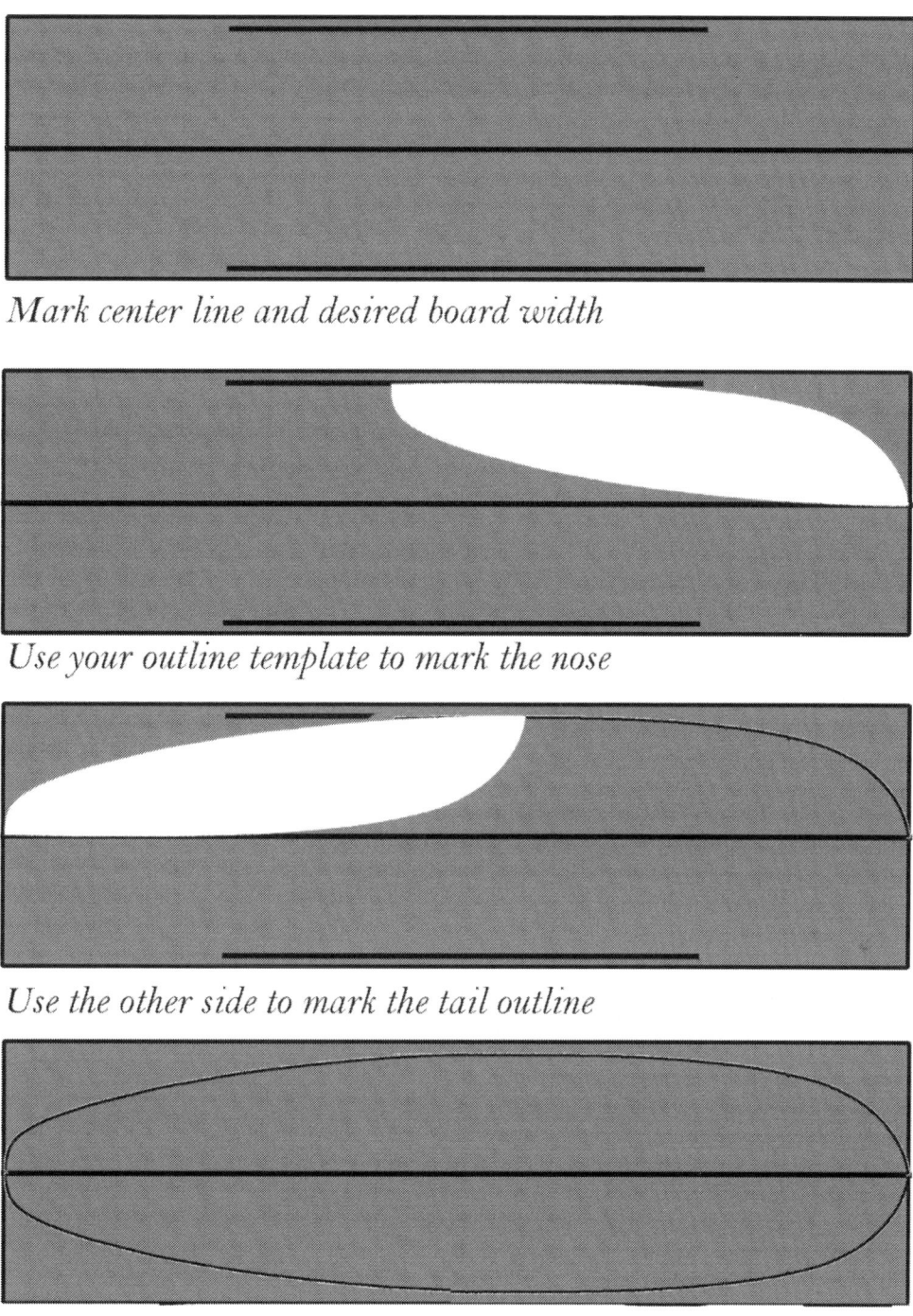

Mark center line and desired board width

Use your outline template to mark the nose

Use the other side to mark the tail outline

Do it again for the other side of the board and you are ready to cut the outline

It's hip to be square

Truing the Bottom Deck
(see illustration, step 2 on page 14)

Now we need to remove some of the stock from the deck and the bottom of the blank to smooth it out and square it up. Let's start with the bottom and get it all to flow down the length and stay nice and level across its width. We will be using our powered hand planer (or a belt sander if you have a lot of spare time). These can be very dangerous to you and your project. One small slip can take off a finger, or worse yet, dig a ditch in your rail (OUCH!) If you are not comfortable with your power planer, just use it to rough in the large areas and then trim away with your block plane (or your belt sander).

Start by taking off any obvious high spots. Look over your blank and find the lowest dips and determine if they will be a problem and make a game plan, dependent on what HAS to happen to get your blank squared up. Is there a twist in your blank? Does one side of the nose or tail pop up or dip off sharply? Do any of these boards need to be realigned and re-glued? If so, pop the glue tack apart and move the offensive board to the proper place. OK, now slowly plane the bottom of the blank until it flows from nose to tail and it level across its width, from nose to tail.

Do NOT worry about spooning the nose or vee in the tail yet, we just want a level surface to build off of. Look, feel, measure, and calculate before you remove stock. Don't be in a hurry to be a failure. Get it as close as you can, we will be going back and finishing it later. Are we having fun yet? Good!

Truing the Top Deck

Now it's time to get your top deck all squared off. Use a pair of saw horses, shimming the legs until the tops of the saw horses are level, then lay your blank across them, deck side up making sure that your bottom surface sits flat on BOTH of the saw horses. Now we're getting somewhere. Take off any obvious high spot in the deck with your planer. Use the same techniques that you used to true the bottom and get that deck trued up. The nose can get tricky if it has a lot of rocker; it's hard to plane a concave surface with a flat planer. You can take stock off easier in these difficult areas by angling your planer or use a spoke shave if you have one. Measure the blank thickness around the perimeter to ensure both sides are symmetrical.

Once the deck is flat and the blank is symmetrical, we can go in and trim the rails down to give the deck some "dome", but keeping the rails blocky and square. Those rails will be taken care of later. Do a couple cuts with the power planer down one side of the deck, then duplicate those cuts on the opposite side. Repeat this to keep your blank symmetrical as you remove stock from the deck until you get the rails blocked to the desired thickness. Keep an eye on the edge of the board, paying close attention to the thickness of the blocked rail, being sure that the thickness flows smoothly from nose to tail. Again, feel for it, measure it, eyeball it, then cut. Remember, we are just roughing it so it doesn't have to be perfect AND we still need some stock left on the blank to smooth it back out after we bust it apart, chamber it, and re-glue it.

It's hip to be square Pt 2

Smoothing the Outline

Now would be a good time to smooth the rough outline of your blank. Remember those lines that you marked earlier using your nose and tail templates? Are they still there? If not, mark them again and we'll get it done. Try to trim the perimeter to smooth the edge, making it flow with these reference lines and remove any wobbles. You can get it real close to the desired finished outline, but leaving a little stock on doesn't hurt. When planing this edge, I find it easiest to knock the large bumps off with the power planer and then finish with my hand planer (or belt sander).

Watch the grain of the wood; it is usually easiest to work from the middle section of the board, planing toward the nose, then from the middle again, planing toward the tail. All you have to do is square it right off, 90 degrees from your nice smooth bottom surface. Again, look, measure, feel, then cut. Those shavings sure do smell good, don't they?

Rough the Rails
(see illustration, steps 3 & 4 on page 14)

You can now make a 45 degree chamfer along the rails. You only need to remove rail stock from the middle of the deck and middle of the bottom; you will round the nose and tail last, so just make it flow until the "points" or "bevels" of the 45 surface ends about a foot from the nose and tail. Look down the rail edge and make sure that the surface of your 45 cut flows well and proportionately with the outer edge.

An easy way to judge this is by looking at the rail thickness as it flows from nose to tail, being sure that it smoothly and gradually tapers as it extends fore and oft. Good enough? Ok, now let's get chambering!!

Roughing the Rails

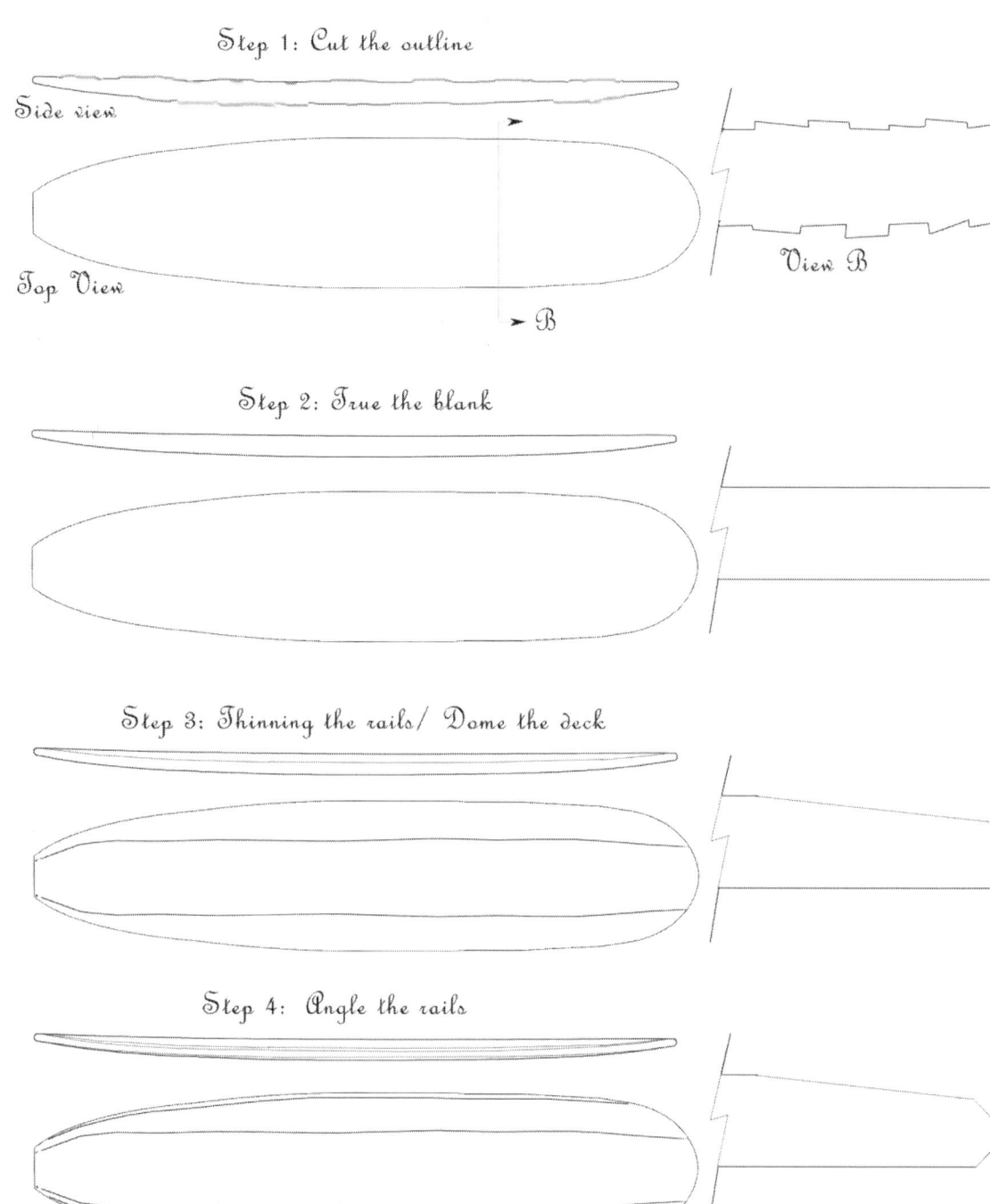

Step 1: Cut the outline
Side view
Top View
View B

Step 2: True the blank

Step 3: Thinning the rails/ Dome the deck

Step 4: Angle the rails

Break It Up

Undo the glue

Breaking the blank back apart can take a bit of time and calculating. Some pieces will come apart with ease, while others will take a bit of convincing to loosen their grip on each other. A rubber mallet can help, just be sure to hit nice and square with the surface and try to hold the blank up while you hit it to avoid any dents from your saw horses or work surface. Avoid using anything as a prying device, it will squish the stock and leave nasty tool marks. If you get a REALLY stubborn bond, you may have to get creative. If you can get one end to part but not the other, try to fish a chisel or wide screwdriver in from the open end and slide it towards the back, touching only the inner surface. Be careful, this will invite splits and cracks. Take your time.

Lighten the load (Chambering)
(see Illustration on page 16)

We need to remove some stock from the inside of this blank to make this log a bit more manageable. Decide what tools you have to use and plan your attack. Check out the diagrams for more info. Using a few different hole saws and then a jig saw is probably the easiest method. If you will be using a forstner bit, go very slow to avoid splits. Drill your holes and then cut between them with a jig saw to remove the large chunk of stock. If you don't have a hole saw of any sort, you can use a small drill bit in all four corners of each chamber and then cut between them with your jig saw. If you don't have THAT you can use a router to CAREFULLY cut out each chamber. If you *only* have a hole saw, just drill a series of holes along the length of each board.

As far as the chamber layout goes, I recommend staggering the chambers, alternating their placement on each board (see diagram) as this allow larger chambers to be cut, since the neighboring chambers can support each other's mid-section. This will allow for a 12-14" chamber to be cut out, as opposed to a 6-8" section in an aligned chamber layout. If you are planning to install a modern fin box, I recommend leaving that section of the board un-chambered. The seam of the fin box can crack and this is a common happening on most all boards. If you were to have a chamber right next to the fin box, it can take in water and start warping, swelling, and eventually rotting of your beautiful board. So leave that stock around the fin box!!! If you plan to glass on fins you can go crazy and chamber the entire length of the board. Be sure leave extra stock in the nose if plan to "spoon" the nose, the same applies to the tail section if you plan to make a vee or concave or any other crazy dynamic features.

Need to Vent?

Are you going to install a vent? In most cases, you won't need a vent but if you plan to neglect your board and leave it in the sun, or take it from extreme cold to extreme heat then you might need a vent (and a good talking to about taking care of your stuff). Decide where you want to place said vent and be sure to mark where the chamber is so you can tap into it. More on the vent installation later.

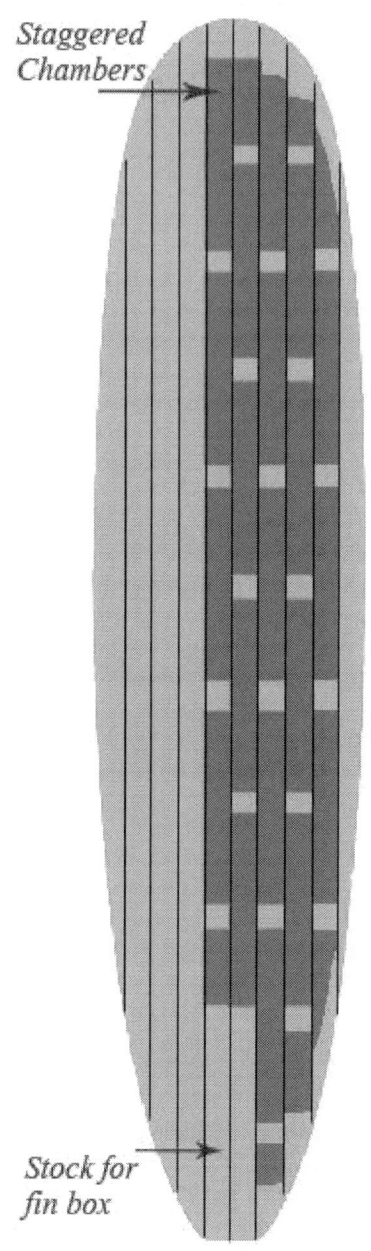

Chambering

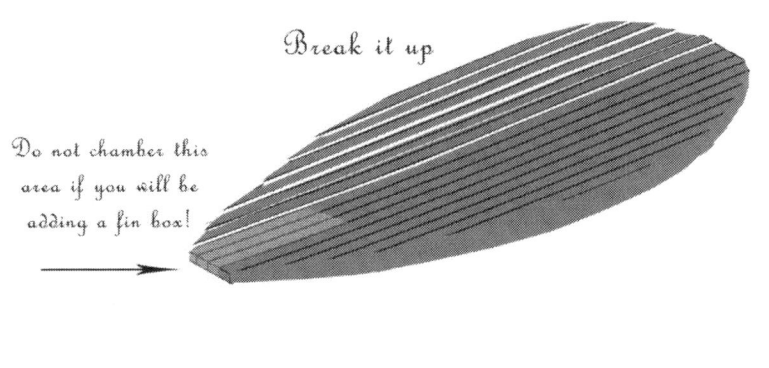

Break it up

Do not chamber this area if you will be adding a fin box!

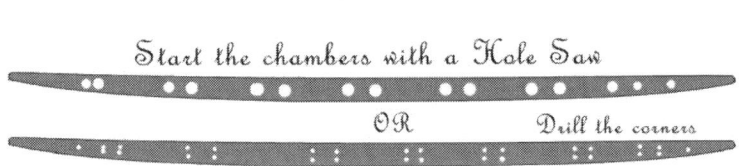

Start the chambers with a Hole Saw

OR Drill the corners

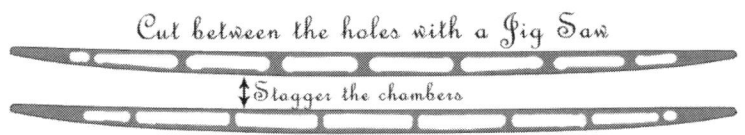

Cut between the holes with a Jig Saw

↕ Stagger the chambers

Then,
    Carefully glue them back together...

Notes

Together Again

On your mark...

Now is a great time to mark out the allowable area for the box placement so you know where you have stock to place it. The same goes for your vent (if you need it) and leash plug placement. Double check your marks since this is your last chance to see your board's inner workings. Make sure there is enough stock to encompass the entire fin box or leash plug, since a hairline crack that normally occurs on any surfboard, can cause you wood surfboard to take on water and start warping or rotting. If there isn't enough stock, just glue some extra stock in there or fill any gaps with thicken resin. After you get that taken care of, go through and inspect each board. Look for any lumps bumps or glue clumps that might inhibit the boards from mating together nice and flat. Smooth them out if you find any.

Go get your clamps, Gorilla Glue, spray bottle, and rubber gloves; it's time to put your blank back together.

Start by grabbing the 2 center boards. It's best to glue 2 boards together at a time, after some practice you might be able to do 4 at a time, but any more than that and you will have some trouble with the boards slipping out of alignment when you are clamping them. Set them together and test clamp them together, make sure you have everything you need to clamp them so you don't have to worry about the glue curing before you get it clamped! If your clamps have small contact area (like the screw type) you may been to use a buffer board along the edge to evenly distribute the clamping pressure. Once you have that all in order, take the clamps off and lay your 2 boards so the mating surfaces face up. You will spray one of the surfaces lightly with water, and then run a bead of glue on the other board, using your gloved finger to smooth the glue enough to cover the entire surface. Now tip them up and slap them together. Use a bar clamp at the tail, snugging it lightly together, line up the seam, then tighten. Next clamp the middle, then the nose, lining up the seams as you move. Add more clamps along the length of the board to keep the mating surfaces nice and tight while the glue cures.

Once the glue kicks, do it all over again on the next pair of boards, working from the center out. When you get to the last few boards on the outside, you might have issues trying to clamp these tapered surfaces. If that is the case, you can wrap a racket strap around the board and squeeze these parts together. I have heard of folks using regular plastic wrap in the same manner, twisting it as you wrap until it squeezes into place. Just be careful not to glue the straps to the board in the process!

That wasn't so hard was it? Now take all those clamps off and scrape those blobs of glue from the seams. Using your planes and sand paper, finish smoothing out the rails and add bottom contours if you need to.

Notes

Leash Plug and Vent

Leash Plug

You can get these from a local surf shop or shaper. If you don't have a shop near you, E-bay will have some or you can order them from Florida FiberGlass (see links on page 25). You need to use a router and a bit that's close to the OD of the vent and plunge a hole just deep enough to seat the vent. Glue it in place with gorilla glue and put something heavy on it to keep it from popping out as the glue kicks.

Venting

I like to use a small Zinc anchor that is sold at most hardware stores. It has wood threads on the outside and ¼"-20 threads on the inside, with a large tapered flat top with an Allen wrench hole for torqueing it into place. (see pic) Drill a hole the size of the outer casing, but small enough so that the threads have something to grab. The top of the hole will need a slight chamfer so the top of the anchor sits flush with the deck. Test fit it a couple times to make sure it fits well, then take it out and smear a little glue on it and screw it back in place. When glassing, you can fill the inside of this anchor with wax so no resin gets in, once its finished, you can drill through the glass and remove the wax with a toothpick. You will want to get a ¼"-20 large head nylon bolt to seal the vent off when in use. (see pic) There should also be an o-ring on the nylon bolt, just big enough to slide over the threads. If it is too big it will squeeze out the sides when you tighten it.

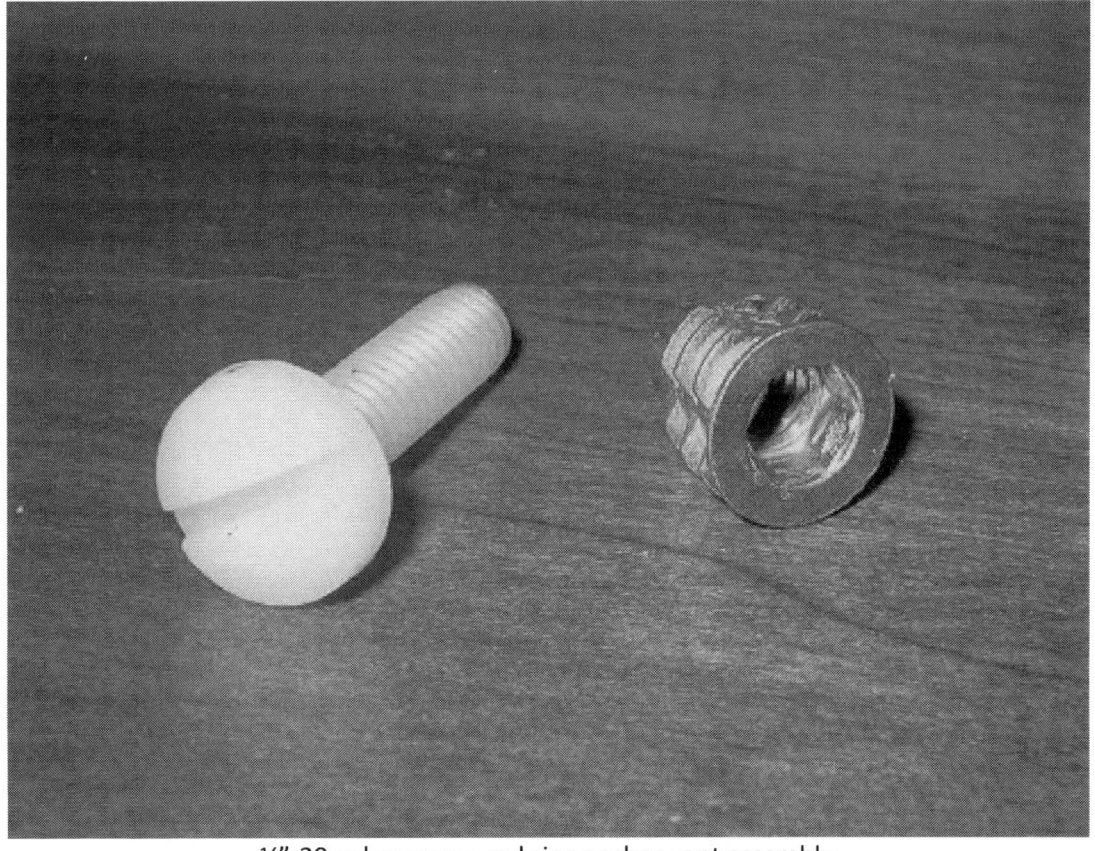

¼"-20 nylon screw and zinc anchor vent assembly.

A Word about Rails

What rails are right for you?

If you are unsure about how to design your rails, you can just go for a nice classic 50-50 rail layout. This is a very usable layout and although there have been a million variations of rail combinations, it will work just fine. Just thin the rails of the board to about 2 to 2.5 inches and taper it into the nose and tail. Then round the rails to a smooth arc, as if there is a round bar running around the perimeter, gradually getting smaller toward the nose and tail.

Finish with a long sanding block to get a nice universal, smooth flow. Likewise, if you are a beginner surfer or if this is your first board, don't worry about the spoon nose and other contours. You won't notice much of a difference. My rocker templates that you use should let you turn just fine too. You can learn a lot about fins by searching Swaylocks forum or check the links that I emailed to you. There are too many factors involved when choosing a fin to cover it in this book, but I tried to sum it up as much as possible in the next section.

Notes

_____

_____

_____

_____

A Word about Fins

What fins are right for you?

If you are unsure about which fin setup you want then you should go for the fin box. That way you can change fins whenever you want, and change your rig for different conditions. I would recommend this since everyone surfs differently and likes different things.

If you are glassing a fin on and want my opinion, go for a standard 8" long board fin, placed so the base is 6-8" from the tip of the tail. The other option is to go classic with a big "D" fin (see page 24) just a couple inches from the tail, but this makes a very "tight" board that won't like turning quickly.

If you are getting the board glassed professionally, the glasser should be able to give you a lot of insight on this and they can even set that fin box in for you when they glass it. They usually have jigs to place fins and boxes nice and square and have knowledge of the local conditions to help you make the decision. If you have the money I highly recommend having your board glassed by a pro. If not, I'll tell you what I know and we'll see what you can do with it!

Mark the center of your board in the tail section and mark the spot where want to place the fin box. Be aware of the thickness of the board along with the height of the fin box, you don't want the fin box to pop out of the top of the board. Once you get that laid out, you can cut out the channel with a router, be careful, the bit tends to pull as you cut. Take it slow, a couple shallow cuts is usually easier to execute than one deep cut. If you are going to use a modern leash plug, now is a good time to use your router to plunge that hole. If you are glassing on your fin, you want to glass the board first.

Glassing

I have glassed my personal boards (chambered cedar) with only epoxy resin, 4 coats, no cloth, and have never had a problem. That said, I would RECOMMEND using at least one layer of 6oz cloth on each side, as it will add a bit of extra weight, but a lot of extra strength. It also gives you a bit more glass to fair out any wonks in the board, smoothing out any wobbles in the finish. See the LINKS on page 25 for more help. If you want to glass yourself, you *need* to go check them out! Regardless, make sure you or your glasser uses a cheater coat (one thin coat of resin on the board before the first lamination) otherwise the board will drink a lot of resin and vent tiny bubbles into the cloth. After the glassing is done you are ready to wax it up and go try it out. Are you ready to build another one? It's the only cure for Wood Surfboard Fever. You can visit TimelessSurfCompany.com for additional info including my guide to building a hollow wood surfboard using a plywood skeleton. In any case, I hope you enjoyed the build. Have fun!

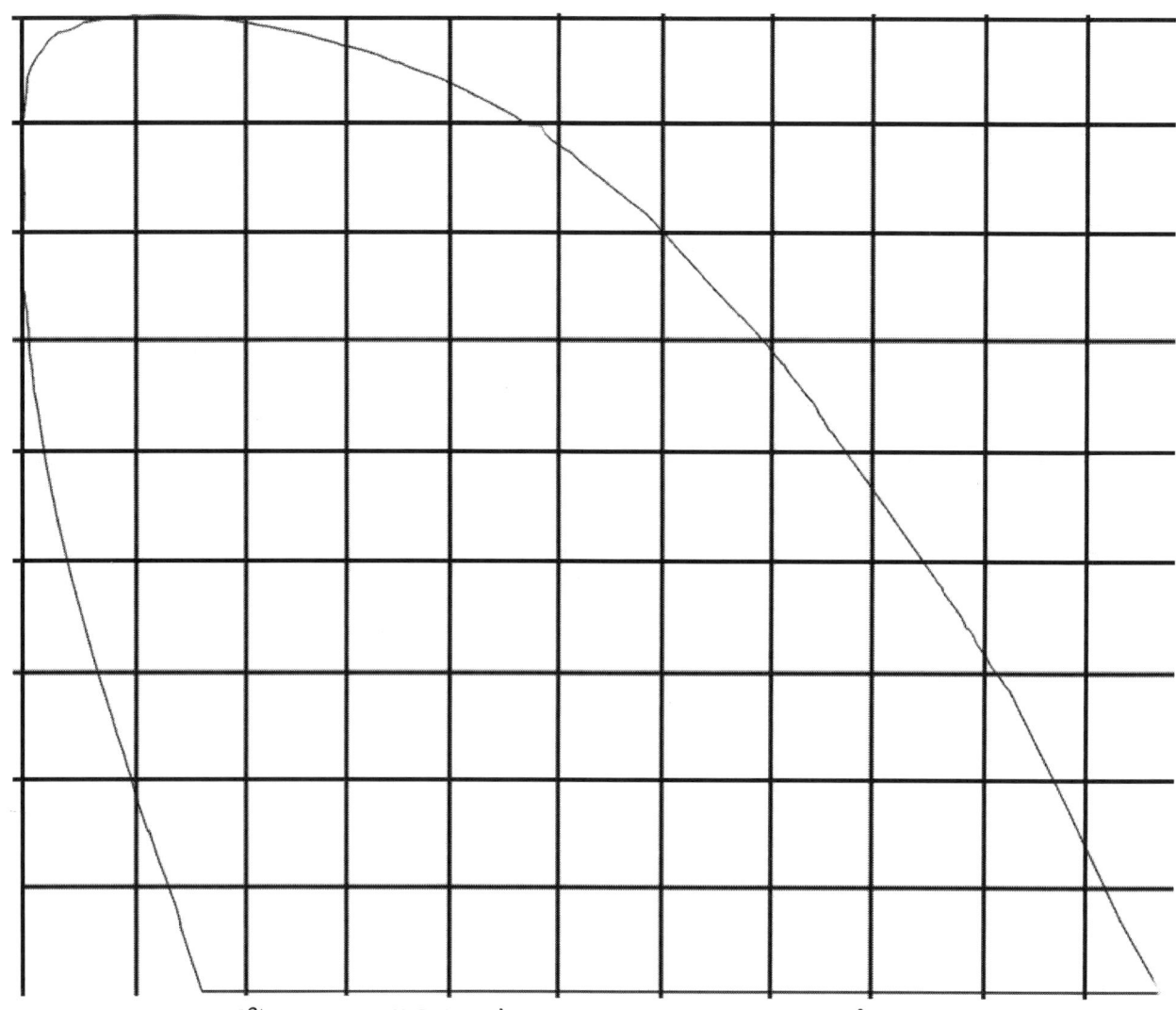

Classic "D" Fin Layout on 1" Grid

Links

Timeless Surf Company
http://www.TimelessSurfCompany.com
http://www.TimelessSurfCompany.com/MyPlans

Wood Surfboard Builders Forum
http://woodensurfboards.proboards.com/

SwayLocks.com
Shapers Forum
http://www2.swaylocks.com/forum

Surfer Steve's
Glassing Info
http://www.surfersteve.com/glassing.htm
Design info
http://www.surfersteve.com/design.htm

Fiberglass Florida
Fiberglass supplies/fin boxes/leash cups
http://www.fiberglasssupply.com/

Closing

Alright, now it's time to surf! Grab your freshly built surf slab, wax it up and hit the beach, being sure to close your vent when you get in the water and then leave it open when you get out (if you added one). Don't leave your board out in the sun heat for long periods of time. Next, close this book by folding it in half, compressing the pages evenly between the covers until the pages can no longer be seen. Keep the book in a safe place that you will remember, just in case you decide to build another chambered wood surfboard.

Thanks again!
Chad

For more information contact Timeless Surf Company at:
www.TimelessSurfCompany.com
TimelessSurfCo@Gmail.com

Made in the USA
Lexington, KY
28 July 2017